God Reminds Me

Nikki Crutchfield

Vol. I and II

Being an assembly of hope in various meters and for sundry occasions

Words N Wisdom Publishing | Beltsville, Md

Nikki Crutchfield/Words N Wisdom Publishing
www.wordsnwisdom.com

Publisher's Note: This is a work of non-fiction. Names, characters, places, and incidents are a product of the author's imagination. Locales and public names are sometimes used for atmospheric purposes. Any resemblance to actual people, living or dead, or to businesses, companies, events, institutions, or locales is completely coincidental.

Book Layout © 2017 BookDesignTemplates.com

God reminds me vol. I & II/ Nikki Crutchfield. -- 1st ed.
ISBN 979-8634679426

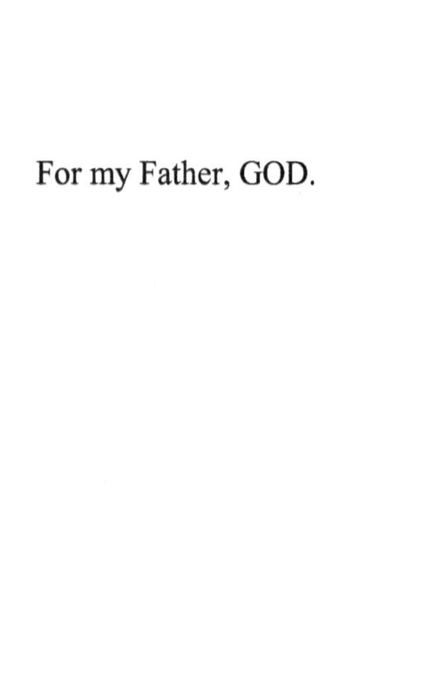

For my Father, GOD.

"My heart is inditing a good matter: I speak of things which I have made touching the king: my tongue is the pen of a ready writer."

—PSALMS 45:1

Vol. I

Oh, He hears you 

GRM by Nikki Crutchfield

A Christian believer is not without negative emotions when faced with difficulties. Oftentimes, we feel overwhelmingly lonely during our most severe circumstances. We may even question whether God sees what we are going through or does He hear our cries for help?

The following story uniquely reveals that God sees and hears us, despite feeling forsaken!

Hagar and her son Ishmael have been cast out the home of Abraham and Sarah (Genesis 21:8-17).

They were forced to wander in the wilderness with meager supplies. Once the bread and water were consumed, Hagar felt desperately hopeless. In her desperation, she decided that she would put her son under a bush to die. As she is yards away weeping and avoiding the imminent death of her child, an

Angel of the Lord appears. He comforts her with the following words: "*What aileth thee, Hagar? Fear not: for*

God hath heard the voice of the lad where he is."

If you read this verse too fast, you will miss the most important part! Prior to the "*Angel of the Lord[s]*" statement, the writer of the text only focuses on the words of Hagar. It would appear that Ishmael is suffering alone and largely abandoned. No one there to hear his weak cries for help, or of hunger. But in the words spoken, God shows that He has both heard and seen Ishmael! God showed up as El Roi- the One who Sees and Hears!

God reminds us, that during trying times we are never alone. He is the God whose eyes and ears are always open to us!

You still have to ask 

GRM by Nikki Crutchfield

Our primary character in 1 KINGS 15:41-43 is a prophet by the name of Elijah. His initial introduction into biblical history begins with a proclamation to the king of Israel (Ahab). He told him that no rain would descend on the earth for the space of three years. After the passing of time, Elijah finds himself once again before Ahab announcing the end of the drought…*"Get thee up, eat and drink; for there is the sound of abundance of rain."*

Immediately following this declaration the prophet goes to pray. Why does he pray *after* his statement of faith?   We'll talk about that in just a second. But, his prayer included:

A Place: "And Elijah went to the top of Carmel." He has created an atmosphere that evokes the memory of a miracle. Mt Carmel is the scene where he won the contest against 850 false prophets. I imagine his mind is mentally engaged on what God did during that moment. Then he gets into…

A Posture of Praise: "and he cast himself down upon the earth, and put his face between his knees." He ends his prayer with worship and thanksgiving.

Elijah prays *after* his faith-filled declaration because he knows that it's not in his power to manifest his faith-filled words- he can't make it rain! Not only does his prayer denote a dependence on God, but how he prays broadens his confidence in Him.

God reminds us, we have to depend on Him to do for us what we cannot do for ourselves!

Not what's gone, but what's left 

GRM by Nikki Crutchfield

2 Kings 19:30 is a prophetic message sent to King Hezekiah from the prophet Isaiah. It is a message of comfort during an extremely intense situation. The Assyrian King, Sennacharib, had invaded the land of Judah and taken 200,150 people captive. He then threatened to come back to destroy the land and to enslave the rest of its inhabitants. With the mentioned text, God promised that the remnant of Judah would prosper again. Specifically, He states— *"they would take root downwards and bear fruit upwards."* What is the significance of this statement, and how do these words convey hope to our lives today?

Many times, the enemy will invade our existence and we can suffer major loss. However, what escapes, and incidentally what we should have left is, our ability to praise! With this simple act of praising God, He will take praise as a seed and cause it to be rooted in the heavens. It then bears up or produces our increase! In other words, our praise has the capacity to make our lives full and complete once again.

God reminds us, praise replenishes after a loss!

What are you hungry for? 

GRM by Nikki Crutchfield

Years ago, there was a very popular ice cream commercial where a variety of people's antics were displayed. These antics demonstrated how far a person would go to have this particular ice cream.

Many professed Christians have insatiable appetites for things that do not increase our spiritual value. We will do whatever it takes to obtain the object of our desire. But in Psalms 42:1 the psalmist encourages us to shift our appetitesour intense cravingtowards God. This craving should resemble the scene as described in the text: A deer who is braying after the essential element of water.

Braying is normally associated with donkeys. The condition of thirst was so great that this animal emits a sound unnatural to its own. What does this mean for us today?

If we are to look "*THIRSTY*" at any time let it be for the longing of the presence of God.

God reminds us, nothing should equal our desire for Him.

This way out

GRM by Nikki Crutchfield

Depression is often referred to as a "dark place." Although a believer has the avenue of Hope in God, we can fall victim to moments of despair.

The writer of Ps. 43 was no exception. His thoughts in verse 2 reveal;

A. He was spiritually depressed.

B. His inner reasoning's of God's whereabouts during his crises.

However, verse 3 reveals his turnaround action- his procession from depression to praise!

What did his turnaround action include? He requests for light and truth to lead him to God's *"holy hill"* In other words, the psalmist prayerfully requested: God illuminate my mind with your faithful deeds. I believe there is a song with the following lyrics:

"When I think of the goodness of Jesus and all He has done for me I can dance, dance, dance, dance, dance all night!"

God reminds us, that we can "think/thank" our way out of depression!

Are you poised for worship? 

GRM by Nikki Crutchfield

Psalms 45 is a wedding song. It is a depiction of the intimate joining between Christ and the church. As we embrace our intimate relationship with Him, it affords us the opportunity to know, independent of how we feel, that Jesus is *"fairer than the children of men."* That He, the Son of God, is more illustrious or notably outstanding than any person we may ever invite into our lives. His acts of love make Him incomparable!

It is this uncommon love that should prompt an unsolicited display of adoration like that of a *"ready writer"* towards Him.

God reminds us, that we should constantly be prepared to offer him praise and worship just for who He is!

It's really true
GRM by Nikki Crutchfield

Psalms 52:8 was written in response to a distressing situation in David's life. He found himself a fugitive on the run from the Mad King (Saul). When questioned by the priest Abimelech, who he has come to for disguised help, he lies to cover his tracks. At the time, this omission of truth appears harmless. But! It results in the deaths of 85 priest including Abimelech's.

Now in a cave, surrounded by men in desperate straits such as himself, David pens Psalms 52. As he is writing, there's a shift that occurs around verse 8. David begins to encourage himself. He metaphorically compares himself to a *"green olive tree."* Why does he make this comparison? David is declaring himself opposite of his reality. As a green olive tree he's essentially believing the following: *"because of my relationship with God, I have a thriving life of excellence!"*

David goes on to become one of the most prominent Kings in

21

Israel!

God reminds us, that His word concerning our lives far outweigh our stark realities.

You can handle the truth 

GRM by Nikki Crutchfield

The Books of the bible encourage the believer to live a life in constant communion with God.

Our communion should include prayer, praise, and worship. Psalms 91 builds on that intimacy by promising protection from demonic attacks. There are many ways this chapter declares how God will protect us, but our attention is being drawn to the latter portion of verse 4"....*his truth shall be thy shield and buckler.*"

What is the connection between *"communion with God" "worship" "protection"* and *"truth"* as it relates to the book of Psalms and particularly this verse? Even though Satan comes with his threatening lies, worship creates an atmosphere where God's truth can be revealed. It is His truth that gives us both stability and surrounding protection.

God reminds us, that worship creates an atmosphere to reveal divine truth!

I did it. I'm guilty. But…

GRM by Nikki Crutchfield

What happens when we find ourselves in precarious situations due to poor choices? Some of us may fear that God will leave us stranded in our circumstances.

That is no different from how the children of Israel felt.

They found themselves forced into exile, and stripped of the familiar….all because of bad choices. They thought themselves forever abandoned by God. However, He says to them in Isaiah 43:1 to *"fear not"* because he has *"redeemed"* them and *"called'* them *"by name"*. Additionally, God declares ownership of them by stating, *"Thou art mine."* God is letting them know that they have not become strangers because of where their decisions have landed them. He remembers who they are because they belong to him, and he is willing to redeem or deliver them.

Face forward

GRM by Nikki Crutchfield

The prophet Jeremiah finds himself being commissioned by God. He felt inadequate and most likely inexperienced because of his young age. God compounds Jeremiah's commission with warning him of the adversity that he will surely face. Although the bible does not reveal how Jeremiah feels about these proposed confrontations, the fact that God has to reassure him gives some indication he is wary of it. With that, God graciously assures him with the following words: *"they shall fight against you, but they shall not prevail against thee: for I am with thee saith the Lord to deliver thee." Jeremiah 1:19*

We may be older or young Christians who are embarking on a new assignment(s) from God. Each new venture has an infancy stage. This young and untried phase is when the enemy is prone to attack the hardest to keep it from coming into fruition. There will be obstacles (possibly in the form of people) that will attempt to impede our progress but if we outlast their attempts, God's words to Jeremiah holds true for us today. *"They may attempt to devour or dispose of you but they will not be able to succeed because I will be there to snatch you away!"*

God reminds us, He's got our BACK. So face and move forward!

What's gonna stop you? 

GRM by Nikki Crutchfield

NIKKI, TONY, AND DAMON IF YA'LL DON'T STOP PLAYING….. I am beating you when we get home". Those were the words we often heard from our mother as a warning to correct our behavior. And no matter how many times we heard/ignored the warning we always acted "dumbfounded" when we were asked to go upstairs to our rooms and await her ARRIVAL….

I believe there are many believers who can attest to the actions my brothers and I took as children. Where we know God is warning us, but we ignore the warnings with a careless shrug as if to say "God's not really going to make me *pay* the consequences." And as a result, we miss out on moments of blessings or encounter unnecessary hardships. This is the constant story of the children of Israel.

In the early verses of Jeremiah chapter 5, we read the outcry of the prophet against God's people. He is declaring the threatening judgement of God. They are being warned of an enemy invasion that would disrupt their way of living. When we approach verse 25 Jeremiah decrees the following: *"Your iniquities have turned away these things, and your sins have withholden good things from you."*

Sidebar: Not only are they about to be intruded upon, but they are the cause of good things being withheld from them.

What good things is he referring too? In the previous verse, Jeremiah mentions the *"former and the latter rain"*. These were rainfalls in Palestine that occurred in the months of March and April and picked up again in October thru early
December. This rain was essential to the maturation of their crops for reaping. In short, they were missing their season of harvest due to sin….

Message!

Sin will prevent us from being set in a place where we can experience the ABUNDANT FLOW of Heaven!

God reminds us, that a pleasing lifestyle secures me a blessed life!

That's not all folks 

GRM by Nikki Crutchfield

The children of Israel are in Babylonian captivity, and it has been a difficult adjustment for them. They possess the knowledge that not all of their brethren were forced to live as captives. Humans are relatively the same despite the difference in time. We compare our lives to others and think we have it worse than they. This comparison can lead to a "God, that ain't fair" attitude. Well, here is our comfort. God said to His people then, and to us now, the following in Jeremiah 29:11 *"For I know the thoughts that I think toward you saith the Lord, thoughts of peace and not evil to give you an expected end."* Although our lives may not resemble others, or it isn't what we'd like it to be, God's word promises that He has an appointed plan of purpose concerning our future. A future absent of calamity, sorrow, or trouble. Rather, it is a promised future of good things to come.

God reminds us, that our present situation is not our end!!

Just Say it

GRM by Nikki Crutchfield

The story in Mark 11:22, 23 picks up with Peter noticing the fig tree, that Jesus cursed the day before, had withered away from the root. In response to Peter's statement, Jesus says several things two of which will be mentioned here. In verse 22 and 23 Jesus mentions the word Have—

> *In verse 22* the word "have" means to- take hold of or possess. *In verse 23, t*he word "have" means- I will be.

When putting these verses together, Jesus is promising..... If we possess conviction in God's supreme power, then boldly declare anything we need in prayer; the results are....He becomes what we need Him to be!

God reminds us, if we believe it then say it.... Jesus will become it!

Troubled Heart? 

GRM by Nikki Crutchfield

God is always concerned about the issues that his children face. In the case of John 14:1a Christ's disciples were concerned about the news that

A. one of them would betray Jesus and *B.* That He would be leaving them soon.

As Jesus sensed their alarm, He admonished them to not allow their hearts to become troubled.

There are times when we know a negative situation is going to occur. We may attempt to prepare for these uncomfortable changes, but living through them could still prove a difficult feat. Though it seems impossible, it is during these challenging times that we cannot allow our hearts to become troubled. In other words, chaos may be ensuing around us, but our minds,

37

thoughts, and our emotions do not have to be in turmoil. Trust in God can maintain our peace!

God reminds us, that He has it all under control!

Are you clinging? 

GRM by Nikki Crutchfield

The only way our lives will have any significance is by our connection to God. John 15:5 *states "I am the vine, ye are the branches: He that abideth in me, and I in him, the same bringeth forth much fruit: for without me ye can do nothing."*

A vine is considered a climbing plant. It coils around its object and grows upward. A branch is called an offshoot or an extension of the vine. Without the vine there is no branch.

The only way that we will move onward, upward, or forward-in God, is if our relationship with Him is the most significant and cultivated relationship in our life. We will not and cannot achieve spiritual success without Him.

God reminds us, only with him can we do anything out of the ordinary.

An encouragement to faithfulness 

GRM by Nikki Crutchfield

Sometimes, it becomes difficult or extremely challenging to mask our emotions when handling hardships. We may exhibit telltale signs of frustration in our body language, or verbal expressions. So much so, our normalcy of conduct changes.

But Paul instructs Timothy, very implicitly, in 2 Timothy 2:3 not to waver in his constancy. He correlates him to three types of people one of which will be our "God reminds me" moment. In verse three, Paul tells him to: *"endure hardness as a good soldier."* In other words, Timothy, you and I are being encouraged to suffer thru affliction, while outwardly showcasing a positive countenance. Inwardly, we are to maintain an excellent and commendable nature.

God reminds us, it matters HOW we go through.

Vol. II

He's for you

GRM by Nikki Crutchfield

Christian's can enjoy many privileges and promises because we wholeheartedly follow God. Incidentally, no one can prevent these special advantages or benefits he extends towards us.

In fact, Romans 8:31b declares *"...if God be for us who can be against us?"* When we get into the place of having the support of, the backing of, or if God has taken an interest in our well-being.... what person, what darkness from hell can prevail against us? Who, which, or what can cause us to fail to obtain what He has predestined, or preordained for us to have? No one!

Remember! When God is for you....it really doesn't matter who's against YOU!!!!

The permanence of favor 

GRM by Nikki Crutchfield

It is possible, that simply living a life of favor will cause people around you to act/react towards you out of fear and intimidation. It then becomes their sole purpose to disrupt the flow of favor in your life. This was true for the children of Israel. They were simply camping in the plains of Moab when the king, Balak, discovered they were in his territory Numbers 22. He heard of the armies of Israel military prowess and was both fearful and intimidated by them. Balak then decided to seek out an internationally known diviner to curse God's people. However, when Balaam was approached for the task he makes an interesting and powerful statement *"I cannot go beyond the word of the Lord, to do more or less."* In other words, he was saying I do not have the AUTHORITY or the

POWER to override, go pass, go beyond, go through, go over, or go around what God has declared! Whew! That was a mouthful….but let's say it again! This time so the devil takes notice. Because no matter what he tries….he does not have *the authority or the power to override, go pass, go beyond, go through, go over, or go around what God has declared.*

Whatever God has said concerning your life…..it is protected and permanent!

Know who you are 

GRM by Nikki Crutchfield

In Matthew 3:13 we read where Jesus is being baptized by John the Baptist and something extraordinary occurs. There is a divine demonstration and declaration that clearly explains who Christ is. In fact, God officially declared *"This is my beloved Son in whom I am well pleased."*

However, right as Satan tempts Jesus in chapter 4, he seeks to cast reasonable doubt about Christ's identity. He specifically states *"If thou be the Son of God..."* By stating "if" the devil was denouncing God's assured proclamation over Jesus life. He insinuated "who God says you are is only a possibility and not a certainty". As we read the interplay, we find that Jesus was firmly fixed on his identity.

We, as the children of God, must act and respond to the enemy with self-assurance.   We must know who we are in Christendom.

Let's declare the following: I. Am. Certainly. Who God says I AM!!!!

I am a friend of God 

GRM by Nikki Crutchfield

The bible refers to Abraham as a friend of God. The term friend is defined as a favored companion. What positioned Abraham to be considered God's friend? How can we be positioned as he was?

Genesis chapter 15 gives us insight as to why Abraham was counted as God's friend. There is a conversation between the two and Abraham expresses his desire to have a child. God replies by taking him outside to show him the stars in the sky. He proceeds to promise Abraham that his descendants would be as innumerable.

Verse 6 opens with these words *"And he believed in the Lord..."* In other words, as soon as Abraham heard what God promised, he believed or was certain it would come to pass. Our belief, confidence, and implicit trust in God is closely tied to our relationship status as a favored companion!

Take the limits off

GRM by Nikki Crutchfield

Psalms 78 is an historical reflection of God's love and Israel's habitual unfaithfulness and disobedience. Verse 41 is a direct reference to God's response to the Israelites failure to believe him. They were unable to believe He could/would defeat the enemies within the Promised Land (Numbers 14:22, 23)

The psalmist Asaph states that they *"turned back and tempted God and limited the Holy One of Israel."* Because of their lack of faith, they limited or they restricted the miraculous power of God from operating on their behalf. They disallowed him from doing *for them* what they could not do for themselves.

Our faith in God releases his limitless power in our Life!

The art of being discovered 

GRM by Nikki Crutchfield

Going after God is the surest way to get discovered…..

John the Baptist points out Christ *"Behold the Lamb of God"* as he is walking by, on two separate occasions, in John 1:2942. The second time around two of John's disciples decide to follow after Jesus. Sensing their presence, he turns to them and asks what are they seeking after? To which they answer with the following: *"Rabbi, (which is to say, being interpreted, master where dwellest thou?"* After spending the remainder of their day with him, Andrew looks for his brother, Simon, to tell him the good news...they have found the Messiah! Upon hearing his brother's proclamation, Simon eagerly follows his brother to see this discovery for himself. His curiosity leads to a profound discovery indeed. Not only does he discover "The Christ" but there's another revelation waiting to be revealed.

When Simon, or Peter as he is commonly known, gets in the presence of Jesus, Jesus *"Beheld him [and] said, thou art Simon the Son of Jona, thou shalt be called Cephas which is by interpretation a stone."*

When we go after God, without a hidden agenda, he reveals who we are and he does so openly. He sets the stage for our discovery!

We know that later in Peter's life, he becomes a stable and key component of the church's inception.

What to do about whisperers

GRM by Nikki Crutchfield

Ever been the subject of conversations? In a bad way? And the words spoken motivated unkind and unprovoked actions? Well, we've all been there. The result of my instance resulted in a heated (very heated) argument between me and a former supervisor. I said some things that shortly left me without employment.

I'm sure I'm not alone in verbal self-defense. We feel justified to correct comments that are made unjustly to us or about us. However, our comments become fuel for the fire and the fire then rages out of control. The Psalmist in Psalms 119:23 experienced a similar predicament but he shares with us a better remedy.

"Princes also did sit and speak against me: but thy servant did meditate on thy statutes."

Alternatively, instead of sparing any thought to the unjust words of others, he focused on and became mentally engaged with the Word of God.

Here's something to remember. When we think, or meditate on His Word concerning us, no other words about us matter!

Now entering the age of fearlessness 

GRM by Nikki Crutchfield

As a kid, I was never afraid of heights. I would climb the tallest trees, or jump from high ledges without a hint of hesitation. But, the older I became the more caution I exhibited. Now, I will climb a tree with proper motivation (being chased by a dog) but will only go so high. I won't jump down a flight of steps *unless* there are only two steps between the take off and touch down points.

I am not sure what occurs in our psyche the older we get, but we seem to lose that hint of fearlessness. And for many of us, the absence of fearlessness causes us to hesitate in moving to higher ground in God. Or, it takes a whole lot of prodding and promises from Him in order for us to take those next steps.

In the first chapter of Joshua, God spends the principal amount of time strongly encouraging him to move into his assigned place. I questioned why? Especially when I looked back at Joshua's earlier years and he appeared to exude a sense of fearlessness….

He was born a slave, but is a conquering commander in

Israel's first battle against the Amalekites at Rephidim.

Shortly thereafter, he is mentioned as being Moses' minister. And Joshua is one of two spies, out of a total number of twelve, who comes back with a courageous and victorious report about their promised land. But as we forward through the years of wandering, Joshua, at the age of 85, has now taken up where Moses left off. During this succession, we can sense the presence of apprehension with God's oft repeated phrase *"be strong and of good courage"*. This leads to my earlier question….why? As I studied for the answer there arose two possible reasons. 1. Could his age or the passing of time have played a part? Did Joshua feel too old to take on this awesome task? Or 2. Was it an inferiority complex-he had some big shoes to fill?

Joshua was both younger and in the background as he assisted

Moses and watched as God used the Exodus Deliverer in a

62

powerful way. Whatever the case, Joshua seems in need of some encouragement and he finds it in the instructions divinely spoken to him *"Be strong and of good courage; be not afraid, neither be thou dismayed: for the Lord thy God is with tee whithersoever thou goest"*.

We have the right to bc FEARLESS! The strength of our success is secured in the Power of God!

Elevation, God, and You 

GRM by Nikki Crutchfield

I wasn't the best student most of my formative years. I had teachers who wanted the best for me and would set an environment conducive for me to learn, but I didn't take advantage of it. I wouldn't do my part, which lead me to taking ninth grade English in the twelfth grade.

God creates the perfect environment for our advancement, but our progression requires partnership with him. We often miss opportunities because we fail to do our part.

> David's life is an inspiring story of how important partnering with God is, when achieving His divine purpose for our life.

Samuel is mourning the rejection of Saul as king, but God has moved on and selected his replacement (1 Samuel 16:1). Later, Samuel arrives at his destination with the purpose of selecting

Israel's next king, and he is confident of God's choice (1 Samuel 16:6, 7)

However, God's choice turns out to be the runt of the litter (1 Samuel 16; 11, 12) Next, God sets in motion a series of events that display David's gradual elevation to his kingly assignment. The dispossessed king is tormented by an evil spirit. His servant's suggest a musician that is skilled in playing their national instrument (the harp) to soothe his troubled mind. The person suggested happens to be the same person that God has just anointed as Israel's next king. Now, although God has set this in motion for David, David has assisted in his elevation by being;

A. Content and committed to his lowly position as a shepherd
B. Passionate about his pursuit of God. He didn't just play the harp but played skillfully-with concentrated effort- in his worship to an audience of One.

Private preparation lends support to our being divinely elevated.

Do you have unfinished business? 

GRM by Nikki Crutchfield

Have you, like myself, ever started a task and left it unfinished? Several little ventures still awaiting our attention, because something or someone has interrupted our progress? Exiled Jews have returned to their homeland of Jerusalem. One of the exiled, by the name of Zerubbabel, has rallied these Jews in order to rebuild Solomon's temple. In the midst of their rebuilding, they encountered *"adversaries"* who attempted to masquerade their true intent as support. Although, their offer to "help" was denied, they would succeed in stopping Zerubbabel. For years to follow, the construction of the temple sat unfinished.

Enter Zechariah's prophecy listed in Zech. 4. God promises the following concerning Zerubbabel:

1.	*"Then he answered and spake unto me, saying, this is the word of the LORD unto Zerubbabel, saying, not by might, nor by power, but by my spirit, saith the LORD of hosts." 4:6*

2.	*"Who art thou, O great mountain? Before Zerubbabel thou shalt become a plain: and he shall bring forth the headstone thereof with shoutings, crying, Grace, grace unto it." 4:7*

3.	*"The hands of Zerubbabel have laid the foundation of this house; his hands shall also finish it; and thou shalt know that*

the LORD of hosts hath sent me unto you." 4:9

In other words, no other resources would aid in the completing of this work. Only by the Spirit of God would Zerubbabel be successful. In completing this task, God would ensure that no obstacle would or could stand in his way. His unfinished business would finally be resolved!

Today, our hope lies in the fact that nothing has to prevent us from completing our goals.....if God is our Finisher!

Don't let the thorns deter you 

GRM by Nikki Crutchfield

Years ago, my aunt grew a rose bush on the side of our house. I remember being drawn to the fragrance and sometimes plucking the roses. What woman doesn't want a rose every now and again? However, I would often hesitate before sticking my hand in the bush because of the thorns. But my desire to have a rose, and to enjoy the fragrance of one, far outweighed my fear of being stuck.

In life, we want to enjoy the fragrant beauty of God's promises. But the thorny obstacles…not so much.

Let's look to Joshua and the wall of Jericho.

One of the descriptive terms of Jericho means

Fragrant-something pleasant to be enjoyed. But Jericho was also the most formidable city. A "thorny" obstacle in the way of God's promise. So there's something pleasant for Joshua and God's people, it's just a little out of their reach! Does he

71

hesitate? Possibly. Is he apprehensive? I'm sure. Does he stop and turn away refusing to go forward? Absolutely not! We know and read in Joshua chapter 6 the walls fell down flat!

With that, let me remind you. Don't let the pain of process, outweigh the pleasantness you will experience when reveling in your promise!

Keep pushing

GRM by Nikki Crutchfield

Back in the day we used to play a game called King of the Hill. The details are a bit sketchy, but here is what I remember: there are a number of people at the top of a hill, while a larger group is at the bottom. When it was time, those at the bottom ran up and the goal was to avoid getting knocked back down. Your opponents were not only those standing on to top, but sometimes, the people climbing the hill with you were your opponents as well. It was an absolute free for all with one goal in mind….get to the top.

In life, perseverance is key. We have to maintain our dogged determination to survive amid those looking to stop us at the top. These are people who want to make no room for our arrival. And then, there are those climbing beside us, who want to beat us up to the top. We must learn to embrace anyone assisting to our destination thru aggravation. It is that tension that makes us strong. Remember that game just mentioned? No matter how many times I got knocked down, I learned my opponents and eventually I was Queen of the hill. Scripture gives a descriptive look into the life of Israel's second king, David (1 and 2 Samuel). His journey to the top was fraught with opposition, but it is through that tension he is tempered into a leader and eventually becomes King of the Hill.

A lesson from Job 

GRM by Nikki Crutchfield

Imagine the following:

Mary was a very manageable child. She always listened to her parents and acted morally correct. As a result, her parents were always bringing home toys and treats for her. One day while playing with her newest doll, Mary's mother stalked in and abruptly snatched her toy away. Mary looked up in utter confusion as her mother angrily said "you're in time out! Get in the corner." Confused and sad, Mary silently rose and slowly walked to face the corner. What could Mary have possibly done? The answer? Absolutely nothing. She was simply the victim of unfair treatment.

It would be reasonable, to the casual observer, to expect a temper to erupt from Mary, or some expression of outrage to occur. But our young miss reverently accepts the actions towards her maintaining her ever-present moral conduct.

This fictitious story is similar to that of Job.

Here is a man who the bible describes as being perfectmorally correct, fears or reveres God, and escheweth-turns aside from evil. As a result of his efforts he has a blessed life. Suddenly everything turns on its head, and one after another fatal situations occur. In the end he is left with nothing but misery. What could Job have possibly done to have all this come upon him? The answer? Absolutely nothing! However, what is unique about his story is the side conversation occurring in heaven. It gives us a clear glimpse as to the real reason behind the havoc. Satan has challenged God concerning Job. He implied Job's love and allegiance to God was a result of bribery; God gave Job good things in order for Job to be the righteous man he was. He insinuated that Job's plush lifestyle was his sole motivation for loving God. God knew this to be in error, but to make Satan choke on his fallible accusation, he allows Job to be tested, a very rigorous testing at that. And Job, unaware of what is taking place behind the scenes, maintains his ever-present integrity. I believe there are some of us who are actually living to the best of our abilities. We are striving for absolute moral conduct. When posed with the proposition to sin we turn away from it. We fear or reverence God. Yet and still we can experience unprovoked serial attacks. Causing us to question "why serve God to such an extent, if unfairness is the result of my efforts?" But….let's imagine for a moment that what we see with Job isn't the first or last of Satan's attempt. That he still comes before God, falsely accusing the saints as detailed in Revelations 12:9, 10. With this in mind, it should make standing through our test easier.

Here are some other points to consider:

God is in control. - Satan goes as far as God allows.

We are given the opportunity to learn how strong we are.

God knows the extent of our capabilities, but do we? We partner with God to prove Satan WRONG! There is nothing sweeter, than gaining a WIN against the devil! If we take this testing full circle, what's lost God gives back in double! Read the end of Job's story!

God is reminding us to maintain our integrity no matter what.

A problem and a promise 

GRM by Nikki Crutchfield

In 1 Samuel chapter 17 a young David has been sent by his father to check on the well-being of his brothers. He has been instructed, by his father, to bring them some vittles. While completing this errand, he finds Israel's army in a quandary. There's a giant threatening his fellow countrymen!

At this moment, God has provided a situation where David has the opportunity to make an unforgettable mark on his way to destiny. David volunteers to face the giant…alone. A short while later, David walks into a narrow passageway to meet his challenge head on. There's no turning back. We know that David not only followed through with his decision to meet the problem, but he ran to meet it!

God reminds us that while the purposes of life are troubled with problems, the problems are only there to reveal His power to and through us!

When I need help believing 

GRM by Nikki Crutchfield

When God reveals his expectations for your life, it's sometimes hard to accept. You ask yourself the question "He wants me to do what?" We determine the request is both, too far out of our league and beyond our capabilities. As a result, many of us never move on what God has asked us to do. The bible tells the story of a young girl who plays a major role in God's overall plan for mankind.

The request is mind-blowing.......

Luke 1:26-27 is the interplay between the angel and Mary the mother of Christ. He has approached Mary to state the incredible to her. What he says goes against the very law of nature. The expectation is for her to understand and accept the impossible. Her response to him shows her struggle to believe:

> *"....how shall this thing be seeing that I know not a man?"*

The Angel explains that God is going to perform the miracle then adds a little extra by way of convincing her. He gives her a tangible point of reference to how God has already done the miraculous:

>*"And, behold, thy cousin Elisabeth, she hath also conceived a son in her old age: and this is the sixth month with her, who was called barren."*

He is letting Mary know God has already done the unlikely and her cousin is a visible representation of the miraculous power of God. He confidently ends the conversation with the following statement:

>*"For with God nothing shall be impossible."*

Shortly thereafter, the bible says Mary made haste through the hills to her cousin's house. I imagine her visit was prompted by curiosity and the need to confirm the angel's words. The moment she enters the house, not only were his words confirmed, but Elisabeth prophetically endorses the birth of the promised messiah through Mary!

Remember, His word concerning you may sound inconceivable, but it's not impossible!

Mission Impossible? 

GRM by Nikki Crutchfield

Has there ever been a moment in your life, when you felt overwhelmed with the many facets of who you are? Fulfilling positions that you were chosen for and consequently accepted? Believe me I know! Before you stands a mother, wife, aunt, cousin, sister, confidant, a minister, teacher, dramatist, writer and well….the list could go on and on. And while attempting to successfully juggle all these positions, the enemy makes every attempt to thwart me through sometimes petty and, at other times, vicious attacks. And the expectation is to do the opposite of Stopping. Dropping. And Rolling out!!

If so, how are we supposed to #CARRYON?

The Bible is filled with stories of people who were just like us and Paul was such a person. How did the Apostle Paul endure being a man who was beaten, stoned, hounded by his enemies, and imprisoned and at the same time, successfully complete his life's mission? He shares the answer with the church at Philippi in Philippians 4:13 *"I can do all things through Christ which strengthens me."* With this statement Paul emphasizes two things when he says the following:

   "I can do" -a greater strength

"through Christ" the Anointed One

In other words, Paul is stating his ability to both handle the responsibility of his varied tasks and endure his hardships was the direct result of his relying upon the Spirit of God.....on the inside of him. This reliance endued him with greater power to succeed!

Just Remember, we "can do all things" through HIM!

Pushed to the limit and *beyond* 

GRM by Nikki Crutchfield

There is a right way and a wrong way to handle provocations. When I was younger I used to watch a show where the main character turned green whenever he became upset. Throughout each episode he attempts to keep a reign on his temper, but eventually he is provoked to the point where he unleashes the monster within. After he comes to himself his clothes are torn to shreds and limply hanging off his body. I watched as he looked around and surveyed the devastation left in the wake of his angry actions.

Can you relate to getting beyond a limit of toleration and turning explosive? Creating a more damaging situation? The woman in 1 Samuel chapter 1 shows us how to handle being provoked and the benefits of a proper response. A husband has two wives by the names of Hannah and Peninnah. One is barren while the other is not, which creates a sort of rivalry between the two women. Peninnah, the one able to bear children, takes any opportunity she can to sorely provoke Hannah who cannot. In fact, the bible calls Peninnah her "adversary" who provokes Hannah in order to make her "fret".

The term "fret" means to be violently irritated. This violent irritation is likened to the sound of crashing thunder. Now, the bible does not say how long Hannah endured this treatment, but it was possibly the same length of time Penninah bear their husband several children. With Hannah this upset.... what does she do? 1 Samuel 1:10 depicts her response..."*And she was in bitterness of soul, and prayed unto the Lord, and wept sore.*" Although Hannah is grieved, she is pushed to petition God and pours out her complaint to him with favorable results. God *"remembered Hannah"* forever silencing Peninnah.

Keep this in mind, only allow negative People to push you to the Point of Petitioning God.

No Pain, no gain

GRM by Nikki Crutchfield

My husband and I made the decision soon after having our second son to cease from having additional children. This permanent choice was due to several factors: pain, discomfort, disappointment, pain, more pain, and did I mention....pain?!! However, that decision left us without the opportunity to ever experience the joys of having a daughter. I let the pain and discomfort of a moment prevent me from ever producing a desired result....having a baby girl.

Is there something you wish to see happen, and want it to occur without hurt and distress? To achieve a goal with complete ease? Most times when this is the case, we either quit in the process or never take the measured steps towards our aim. It is here that we need to be encouraged to be a group of believers that endure!

In Romans chapter 8 Paul, the writer, talks about the sufferings of Christians (vs 17, 18). He follows with examples of suffering in verses 35, 36. But he gives a note of triumph for the suffering believer in verse 37. He says *"Nay in all these things we are more than conquerors through him that loved us."* In other words, it doesn't matter what distress or persecution the believer faces, he is preeminently victorious by leaning to and living through the strength of Christ... who lives on the inside of him!

Our Strength is that close!

Our reminder? We can live victoriously through God's power!

Keep calm and stay focused 

GRM by Nikki Crutchfield

Emotions can run unchecked. I had an unforgettable experience, years ago, where a woman of a different race hurled an ugly insult at me.

Instead of shrugging my shoulders and taking a nonchalant attitude, I allowed my anger to come to a slow boil. On that day I used words long forgotten and perfectly constructed sentences using the language of cuss. I was so consumed by my anger that cussing became insufficient, I needed to do bodily harm. Kindly note this moment in history occurred as I professed being a sold out believer.

While I am being transparent, I believe there is someone reading who can readily identify with emotions raging out of control.

Emotions so consuming that we are not functioning properly. Our focus has been lost and we are not aware of any looming risks!

1 Peter 5:8 states these words *"Be sober be vigilant because your adversary the devil, as a roaring lion, walketh about seeking whom he may devour."* Peter's statement comes at a time where emotions are highly charged. The Roman emperor, Nero, is on a Christian killing spree. To be named a Christian puts a person in the cross-hairs of severe persecution. The believers of that day became overwrought with fear. To counter the contemplation of walking away from their beliefs because of this, he writes these words *"Be sober be vigilant because your adversary the devil, as a roaring lion, walketh about seeking whom he may devour."* Essentially, he is encouraging believers to be both calm and collected in spirit while giving strict attention in restricting Satan access through emotional vulnerability. Because his end goal is "eternal ruin", we must remember to keep calm and stay focused!

You are strong enough 

GRM by Nikki Crutchfield

When I started my weight loss journey, I joined a grueling strength training class. It was something I'd never encountered before. I would often look for the trainer to let me out of prescribed sets. That never happened. In order for me to succeed, something had to click within me. I had to gain and maintain an inner strength.

Most times, we want God to physically remove us from straining situations. Where we do not have to face the pains or disappointments of life. However, instead of eliminating or preventing the issue from occurring He does something equally powerful and effective.

Psalms 138 is a Psalms of thanksgiving where David is expressing gratitude or giving public acknowledgement of God's divine goodness.

This expression of gratitude is clearly seen in verses 1 and 2. The question then becomes what is David so gratuitous about? There are several reasons mentioned but verse 3 will receive our attention. It states:

"In the day when I cried thou answeredst me and strengthenedst me with strength in my soul."

God responds to David's plea by making him bold and full of power and authority. David wasn't moved out of the situation but his mind, will, and emotions were tempered with the strength of God to withstand!

In times of strain remember, He makes us strong enough to endure our TESTS.

When your sacrifice doesn't make sense

GRM by Nikki Crutchfield

For many years my husband and I were youth leaders. We sowed time, money, effort and energy into the lives of many teens. There were times where I felt like it was a waste of time, money, effort and energy. I often questioned myself does my sacrifice make sense? Especially when there were *other things* I could have been doing with my time, money, effort and energy. Are you getting the picture?

I believe, there are many of us who look at the value of what we are sowing *verses* what/who we are sowing into, and not see it is a purposeful endeavor. Consequently, we stop what we are doing and never see the results of what our sowing could have produced in us or in the lives of others.   The following portion of scripture describes the end of a 3 year drought. 1 Kings 17:1 the prophet Elijah makes a pronouncement to King Ahab that there would be no "dew" or *"rain"* till at his word. Between chapters 17 and 18 three years have passed and God told Elijah it was time to present himself before King Ahab. Essentially the drought is over. However, there is a demonstration of God's power before the people in the form of a sacrifice.

During the sacrificial offering, as Elijah faced off against the prophets of Baal at Mt. Carmel, he pours out 12 barrels or portable jars of water on and around the altar. Now this water would have been a precious element during that time because they are in the midst of a drought. So the question that came to my mind, especially if I were watching this take place is, Why is he wasting that water as a part of a sacrifice? Further still – why give up something so precious to be consumed, used up-by someone other than me?

But if we read verses 41-46 of chapter 18 God would pour out from the Heaven's, more than what He consumed in the sacrifice. Verse 45 states *"And it came to pass in the meanwhile, that the heaven was black with clouds and wind, and there was a great rain……"*

Don't stop giving! Our sacrificial sowing will cause us to receive Heaven's abundance.

Reeead

GRM by Nikki Crutchfield

I have always been an avid reader. Reading increases your vocabulary and ability to articulate. Proper articulation prevents frustration. Knowing how to communicate, in any given situation, allows the person to get their point across effectively.

As believer's, reading is essential to our success. Not just any reading material, but expressly delving into and studying the word of God. Ephesians 6:17 states the following:

"And take the helmet of salvation, and the sword of the Spirit, which is the word of God. "

Let's breakdown the highlighted portion into two parts. First he says *"the sword of the Spirit..."* Sword is defined as an instrument that creates death. Spirit is referenced as the third person in the trinity. Next he says *"which is the word of God."*

Put together, the verse says…..the power and presence of God is reflected in His word!

Reading and recounting God's word, during times of spiritual warfare, eliminates any effects of Satan's efforts against us.

I got the power 

GRM by Nikki Crutchfield

Paul arrives to a place in his life where he is troubled on purpose. In 2 Corinthians 12:7-10 we read the following: 7:*"And lest I should be exalted above measure through the abundance of the revelations, there was given to me a thorn in the flesh the messenger of Satan to buffet me, lest I should be exalted above measure."* Despite the reasoning behind the *"messenger of Satan"* sent as a splinter to mistreat Paul, it would appear this persistent harassment became overwhelming for he *"besought the Lord thrice"* concerning it. This translates to mean, he petitioned God three times about eliminating this issue. However, he quickly goes from petitioning God to stating in verse 10 *"I take pleasure in infirmities, in reproaches, in necessities, in persecutions, in distresses."*

What happened? Why did Paul's attitude shift to rejoicing, when previously he suffered from want of strength, mental injury, imposed calamities, and extreme afflictions about his *"thorn"*? Well, in verse nine God assures Paul that

His grace, or favor, will be his unfailing strength. I believe Paul was divinely empowered to endure and outlast his situation by the grace of God.

Fact: We are incapable of being victorious, mentally or otherwise, without Him.

How we worship matters 

GRM by Nikki Crutchfield

A few years ago, I attended the concert of a major performer with my bestie. I was among a large, screaming, singing, dancing crowd of over 2,000 fans. The concert lasted well over two hours, all of which I stood. Not once did I complain about how long he was up there singing. Nor was I bothered by the short break given in between his set, in order to rest a bit. Looking back, I gave a lot to a person who didn't know I even existed. A singer I knew and could recognize, while he couldn't pick me out of a line up. And yet, I didn't think it robbery to give all my energy, or my outlandish display with nothing in return, but a momentary thrill of hearing him sing songs I barely knew!

I have seen people give their all at football games. At the club. Or out in public waiting for a bus....just bopping away. And yet, some of us, who are these same people have the audacity to get perturbed when we're encouraged to reach beyond personal feelings and demonstrate proper oblations of worship to God. Our body language shouts "LEAVE US ALONE"; let me worship God in my own way. But if we're honest, our way involves halfheartedness….at best.   There's no direct focus…. no attention on God, and/or an outright refusal to praise or offer him thanksgiving. Really??! The following scripture depicts a similar attitude.

In chapter one of Malachi, the prophet is reprimanding the priests for failing to meet the expectations of sacrificial worship as detailed in Leviticus 22:21-23. Malachi specifically chides them for presenting, *"polluted bread"* and animals that are *"blind, lame and sick"*. These items were given to them by the children of Israel, in order for the priest to sacrifice on their behalf. In reading, I questioned the following: why did they accept, from the people, what was unacceptable in the first place? Clear about the requirements, why didn't they challenge the people to give God a perfect sacrifice? The answer I arrived to was this…..either they didn't care or didn't think God would mind. Well, the opening verse tells us the *"Word of God"* was a *"burden"* on Malachi, or a heavy concern of God transferred to him. And with that burden, the prophet rightly condemned the priest, the informed leaders, for failing to correct the people's way of worship! Sidebar: It is the duty of our leaders to encourage, instruct, and/or remind us about proper worship. Why? Because failing to do so, puts them in the same position as the leaders of Malachi's day….seemingly un-bothered. To add insult to injury, it would appear they had more regard for a man than God! The latter part of verse 8 declares:

"……..try giving gifts like that to your governor, and see how pleased he is!" says the Lord of Heaven's Armies." They wouldn't think to give blemished animals or polluted bread, as a gift to a man, but without hesitation offered it to God?! God, who had done more for them than any man could or would do! God, who knows them individually and can pick them out of a lineup? A God who can pick out his people from a crowd of millions! You see where I'm going with this?

It is our responsibility, as people of God, to give him our best worship- Proper oblations- words and physical gestures that are honest, pure, and from the heart. Should we fail to do so, there are people that God has placed in our lives to remind us of what proper worship should reflect!

Reader, how we worship Him, matters!

What do you give a God who has everything?

GRM by Nikki Crutchfield

David asked a question in Psalms 116:12 *"What shall I render unto the Lord for all his benefits towards me?"* In other words, he is asking; "what can I give back to God in return for everything He has done for me?" The psalmist is expressing a desire to do something for someone who has everything and needs nothing. We can connect David's opening question of, *"What shall I render?"* to Romans 12:1 *"I beseech you therefore; brethren by the mercies of God, that ye present your bodies a living sacrifice, holy, acceptable unto God, which is your reasonable service."*

Connection? Our exhibition of a holy lifestyle is a fair, logical, and acceptable return for all God's goodness towards us.

Hide and seek 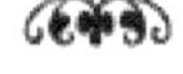

GRM by Nikki Crutchfield

There is a place for every believer, of impregnable strength. A place of refuge and refueling that the bible speaks of, but is concealed or hidden as revealed in Psalms 91:1, 2.

Q: Why would God create a place of rest from the trials, tribulations, and temptations of life... that's secret?

A: He wants us to search for HIM. To pursue after HIM in times of trouble. To go after him with a singleness of mind. Forsaking all other possible avenues or vices or substitutions as remedies.

Success, during life's challenges, depends on our unwavering PURSUIT of HIM!

Where is he? Pt. 1 

GRM by Nikki Crutchfield

The word "in" can be defined with the term "location" which in turn means the whereabouts of a person, place, or thing. We will connect the defining terms of "in" and "location" with Psalms 76: 1, 2 to answer the posing question "Where is He?" Verse 1 states *"in Judah is God known."* Here, the psalmist is referencing an actual location in the southern part of Canaan. Judah is the location where the tribes of Judah and Benjamin reside. It is clear that the writer is sharing that God revealed Himself to His people while in this land.

But the revealing of himself is not confined to the pages and places of the bible. Judah has another Hebrew meaning of praise. The scripture now becomes relevant if we read the verse as such: "In Judah-praise- is God known- or revealed." In other words, He becomes recognizable. A tangible presence to be experienced.

Just a side note: In the atmosphere of praise, our hopes can be built. When His formidable presence is realized, he becomes more concrete than any confusing, distressing, or troublesome situation we may face.

Where is God? At the center of our praises!

Where is he Pt. 2? 

GRM by Nikki Crutchfield

The best way to prove a fact, is to provide undeniable evidence that all claims are true. What fact are we claiming as factual? That God is real. And the reality of His existence is made manifest within the good and bad times we experience as believers.

The latter portion of Psalms 76:1b boldly declares *"....his name is great in Israel."* The psalmist is stating that God has a sizable reputation which proves He not only exists, but that He is a God who prevails for His people. It is this reputation or track record that is repeatedly detailed in the Word of God. Psalms 76 was penned to declare God's triumphs. One such triumphant moment was the defeat of the Assyrian army and King Sennacharib (2 Kings 19:36).

However, God's sizable reputation does not start and end with His word. In the lives of many, if not all Christians, we possess our own testimonies that solidify the reality of God and His power to prevail.

God's tangible existence can be found or discovered in his reputation!

He is the air I breathe 

GRM by Nikki Crutchfield

Genesis 2: 7 states *"and the Lord God formed man from the dust of the ground and breathed into his nostrils the Breath of Life and man became a living soul."* Breath equals life. When we breathe, we breathe earth's natural element called Oxygen. Oxygen is drawn to the earth by gravity. Without oxygen all things living would die. As a matter of fact, oxygen is so vital that four minutes of oxygen deprivation can lead to severe brain damage and even death. For this reason mountaineers and astronauts, those that enjoy going beyond earth's limits, rely on compressed oxygen. Compressed oxygen is gas contained in specific containers, which allows them to breathe or live and enjoy being in the beyond....beyond.

I believe God has destined a good portion of his people for heights unknown, but the key to survival is constantly inhaling and exhaling his presence. He has to be alive in, and oxygenating our very existence. Paul puts it this way in Acts 17:28 *"In Him we move we live and have our being."*

The ultimate thirst quencher 

GRM by Nikki Crutchfield

As believers, there may be moments when we look for physical experiences to satisfy an internal spiritual longing. The following story represents Jesus as the Ultimate thirst quencher. He is referred to as The Living Water.

Jesus was compelled to go through the city of Samaria, St. John 4. Customarily, this was unusual as the Jews had no dealings with the Samaritan people. Why did Jesus feel the need to go through a city that he, by societal norms, should have avoided? One, he was breaking through the pious barrier of the ultra-religious Jews. However, my deeper belief is that, he wanted to help a woman in need of her spiritual thirst being quenched. During their discourse, Jesus instructs her to go and *"call her husband"*. She replies that she does not have one. He then proceeds to pull back the covers of her veiled life.

Jesus states that she has in fact had *5* husbands and the *1* that she is currently with, is not her husband. That would bring her intimate encounters to *6*. And right at this moment she is having another intimate meeting. Although it's of a different nature, Jesus makes man number *7*. Seven is the number of completion. Completion is the state of being whole….with all the necessary parts. We find out that Jesus was her missing piece!

Do you need your thirst quenched, like the woman at the well? Then Jesus is all you need!

The company I keep

GRM by Nikki Crutchfield

The psalmist David makes three definitive, but conjoined statements about God in Psalms 16:11. One of which is *"In thy presence is fullness of joy..."*

David is confidently declaring that being in the presence or company of God will gratify us beyond capacity with joy-gladness or mirth!!

Being surrounded by Him, can make a change in our emotional state!!

Be stumble free 

GRM by Nikki Crutchfield

Did you ever witnessed someone stumble as they walked. Then you notice them look back at the space where they stumbled? I have. And I will go so far as to admit that I have done the same. Most times, I will stumble or miss the fact that I am walking on uneven pavement because I'm mentally preoccupied. I believe mental preoccupation disrupts our ability to pay strict attention to our surroundings as believers. We miss moments where the enemy is subtlety entering our space and before we know it we are tripping headlong into deception and/or a distraction. And it's not until we are picking ourselves up, dusting off dirt, that we stop to consider how we got here....wherever here is.

This is why 1 Peter 5:8 admonishes us to:

"Be sober, be vigilant; because your adversary the devil, as a roaring lion, walketh about, seeking whom he may devour".

In other words, to avoid missteps that can lead to satanic destruction, we have to be sober be alert and vigilant- Watchful.

You didn't know? 

GRM by Nikki Crutchfield

Does this sound familiar?

"I didn't know?" Or, "I forgot?"   I don't believe they "forget" or they "don't know".   You hear this after you question your child or children because they did or didn't do what was asked of them. I believe, they believe, that if they feign ignorance it will get them out of inescapable trouble. I believe they may have gotten away with doing or not doing what was asked for so long…..that they think they are getting away with those actions. Now cries of injustice shatter glass ceilings as they suffer through our choice of discipline. As mature adult believers, we are no different. As long as we have not suffered any negative consequences from certain choices... we will continue, and continue, and continue until our penalties catch up and overwhelm us. And we too, are raising the roof with our cries along with attempting ignorance.

The book of Judges gives a similar story, showing people are the same despite time. The children of Israel were left to enjoy 40 years of rest at the close of Judges Chp. 5. However, at the opening of Judges 6 the bible states "And the children of Israel did evil in the sight of the Lord: As a consequence, God *"delivered them into the hand of Midian seven years."* Somewhere in that seventh year they decided to cry out to him. Now, he does intend to send Gideon as a deliverer, but not before he sends a prophet to explain the cause of their predicament. Why does the prophet need to explain what is evident? If I could be afforded the opportunity to state what I think; I don't believe they were all that ignorant. Chapter 3 shows a pattern of idolatrous worship that led to oppression. They knew what was up! What I do accept as true is the following: because they didn't feel the immediate punishment of their sin, they simply carried on and on and on until well.....God had, had enough. And he used the problem with the Midianites to capture their wayward attention.....again.

So their cries for deliverance should have been preceded by cries of repentance. It may be possible that some of us are in the position(s) that we are in due to poor lifestyle choices. And God is using our storms, stress, and maybe sickness to capture our focus. There is nothing like pain and affliction to redirect our attention back on God and his commandments. Here is the hope of the story. As soon as they called out to God, he answered. Not just with a stern reminder but also with a saving rescuer. In the event you are honestly in doubt or feel absolutely clueless concerning specific pains or discomforts in your life, ask God "what's up?" I GUARANTEE he will answer you. And if he shows you that you're the reason for your dilemma, own it! Ask for forgiveness before asking for the help to get out. Remember, eventually choices and consequences will collide!

Get on the same page 

GRM by Nikki Crutchfield

I became pregnant (before he put a ring on it) while being very active in ministry. Prior to my pregnancy, I received several divine warnings to which I ignored or chose not to believe. I honestly thought "God is not going to let that happen to me" despite what I was doing to ensure it happened. I could say a lot of things to justify my actions-he was my boo, we was getting married anyway, etc…. But the real of it bordered down to me deceiving myself. I knew premarital sex was wrong. I knew God wasn't pleased with my lifestyle, but surely I would be extended grace…. a pardon for my sin….allowing me to escape the consequences.

That was not to be so. He exposed me and the aftermath was horrible.

Many Christians live in a state of self-deception and are unprepared for the results of a sinful lifestyle. Where our actions don't exactly align with God's requirements.

127

This was no different for his people.

Jeremiah states these words, in Chapter 7 verse 8 in the book named after him *"Behold ye trust in lying words that cannot profit"*

The children of Israel believed themselves immune to the judgement of God. They thought all the prophetic warnings they were receiving surely wouldn't come upon them. They believed their being God's chosen people exempted them from the consequences of a sinful lifestyle. In addition to this distorted mentality, the children of Israel found further security in chanting *"The temple of the Lord"*. This mantra kept them locked in religious rituals that failed to encourage righteous living. In other words, as long as they attended church 3 times a year (ritual) but lived as they saw fit (no real relationship with God) they were still okay.

In order to abort this way of thinking, God had the prophet Jeremiah to stand at the door of the temple and prophesy to the people as they entered to worship. Verse 8 specifically records they should not *"trust in lying words"* because they would not *"profit"* from them.

In short, God's people were lying to themselves. They were mired in Self-Deception and he was attempting to get them unstuck before destruction occurred.

Here's a simple reality check: Our truths must align with God's facts. Get on the same page!

To be or not to be Christ-like 

GRM by Nikki Crutchfield

One of my biggest challenges, as a believer, is dealing with people. Specifically the negative actions of others towards me. My unrealistic expectations are that folks will treat me the way I endeavor to treat others. With no hidden agenda or straight out meanness.

When unprovoked attacks occur, it catches me off guard and I respond without thinking at times. Recently, I reluctantly added a coworker as my social media friend. Soon after, she started throwing "shade" my way. Immediately, I blocked her. She asked me one day "so you don't be on social media like that anymore?" I crossed my fingers behind my back and replied "yes".

Unfortunately, she was not my first social media eviction.

My main issue centers around knowing how to immediately forgive others of their offenses towards me, as a CHRISTian should. But there is a way to conquer this spiritual challenge.

Acts chapters 6 and 7 reveals a portrayal of a man by the name of Stephen. This story tells us how we can manage ourselves responsibly. He first endures false accusations. Then, while being fatally attacked, he is quoted as saying these words *"Lord, lay not this sin to their charge"*, after which he peacefully dies. How does Stephen successfully cope with the unprovoked, negative bombardment of actions towards him and remain CHRISTian with his last dying breath? How does he take the similar position, like Christ, in his response? Acts 6:5 gives insight with these words *"And they chose Stephen a man full of faith and of the Holy Ghost...."* The answer to the question lies within these two points: He was FULL of A. faith and B. The Holy Ghost. In other words, Stephen's entire being was permeated with both confidence in his relationship with God and the power of God's spirit. This martyr allowed his faith and the indwelling of God's presence it to be his direct influence of how he lived his life. Including this severe moment he finds himself in.

Our only option at successful CHRISTian living is honoring Christ's position in our life and to be under His direct control.

It will cost you something 

GRM by Nikki Crutchfield

Since I was a little girl I have been fascinated with texture. If a woman wears a fur coat (known to me or not) I will finagle a way to touch it. My mother's oldest sister used to babysit my brother's and me. In addition to us, my aunt Shirley used to watch other children. We were forewarned not to touch any of the other children's things. But there was one who used to come in a car seat. A car seat which had a very thick, off-white, corded strap. When I felt it, I became fixated with the idea of cutting it with scissors. I wanted to see what it would feel like to cut against that corded grain. Although my Aunt's warning rang in my mind, and my day was going extremely well for a five year old, curiosity won out and I cut it. When the question was asked who did it? I along with my brothers innocently declared "I don't know" and "not me". We all got in trouble.

Today, there are many believers whose curiosity gets the best of them. A thought or a satanic suggestion is planted in the mind and germinates until it becomes an action. However, we are never prepared for the assailing and often overwhelming consequences that accompany our disobedience.

The same could be said of a very famous biblical couple....Adam and Eve. These two people had a very pleasant experience pre-sin. They lived in "sinless bliss". Adam and Eve had absolutely no knowledge of the debilitating consequences associated with disobedience. However, once they gave in to the satanic suggestion of eating of the forbidden tree....their post-sin experience resulted in a premature death. I mean they lost out! Their garden style living was abruptly ripped from them.

Sinful indulgences come with an exacting price!

Obedience matters 

GRM by Nikki Crutchfield

There are many...many.....many, many moments when it is difficult for me to do what I am told. Countless times, as a child, my mom told me and my brothers outside was off limits while she was at work. But my desire to do what I wanted often outweighed her instructions. One snow day, I was observing all my friends having fun outside. They were skating/sliding across this thick sheet of ice. I longed to be out there. It didn't matter that I watched them go inside, one by one, I was determined to skate across that thick ice....

After about the third time we skated across, I slipped, fail, and knocked myself unconscious. Next I knew, I was waking up in my living room...no idea how I got there. A tale my mother never knew....gulp, till now. That's only one of many of my willful acts when I was little.

As an adult, I've gotten better, but being completely obedient is still a challenge. Consequently, I find myself embroiled in repercussions that are not ideal. I am sure that I am not alone with acts of disobedience. I am sure someone reading has found themselves doing the exact opposite of what they were expected to do. We are willful at work, at home, in the church and sadly, in our relationship with God. Guess what? We are not alone.

Difficulty with obeying can be traced back to biblical times. There was one such person by the name of Saul.

The following scriptures detail the synopsis and result of Saul's disobedience: 1 Samuel 15:3

~Saul receives clear instructions

1 Samuel 15:19

~Saul's partial obedience

1 Samuel 15: 11

~God's response

God's attitude towards Saul's partial obedience was one of supreme disappointment. Saul's choice indicated that he chose fleshly desires above what God mandated him to do. He's rejected, and stripped of his kingship. Tormented till the day of his death by an evil spirit. If only he'd listened.

Our Obedience Matters.

You can't have the best of both worlds

GRM by Nikki Crutchfield

I find menu options overwhelming. In my mind, I believe there is always something better to eat than what I have selected. So even after I have settled on what I want, I am never satisfied. And I almost always stray to my husband's plate.

The critical problem is a lack of contentment. To be honest, this lack of contentment sometimes spills over into my spiritual life. I find myself attempting to simultaneously please God and fleshly urges. Are you one, like me, who endeavors to live as God requires....but still say, think, and act in ways that are contrary or un-Christ-like?

We're not by ourselves.

The children of Israel had established a practice of being lukewarm. Worshiping both God and Baal.

Sadly, they were divided in their devotions. And because of this indecisive state they are posed with a direct question to which they can offer no response. In 1 Kings 18:21(NIV) Elijah the prophet asks them *"How long do you waver between two opinions? If the LORD is God, follow him; but if Baal is God, follow him. But the people said nothing."*

They didn't respond. However, each day *we* are given the opportunity to offer a reply: Will we follow him wholeheartedly or not?

Kindly note: There are no "gray" areas when serving God.

Things are BLACK and WHITE! Choose a side and stick with it.

The struggle is real 

GRM by Nikki Crutchfield

There is a definitive line in the life of every believer between fleshly and spiritual deeds. In fact, the bible gives a direct list of the two:

List A - Galatians 5: 19-22

Adultery Fornication

Uncleanness

Lasciviousness

Idolatry

Witchcraft Hatred

Variance

Emulations

Heresies

Envying's

Murders

Drunkenness

Reveling

List B Galatians 5: 23

Love

Joy

Peace

Longsuffering

Gentleness

Goodness

Faith

Meekness

Temperance

It is quite clear, upon reflection of these two lists, which one ends with the dire consequence of *".....That they which do such things will not inherit the kingdom of God."* How do we

avoid the manifestations/struggles of List A which will ultimately cost us our place in the Kingdom? The simple solution is found in Galatians 5:16 *"This I say then, Walk in the Spirit, and ye shall not fulfill the lust- the intense cravings- of the flesh."*
The success of Christian living depends on the level of divine influence we allow.

Dare to be different 

GRM by Nikki Crutchfield

A person who goes against the grain, refuses to be a part of the norm. And as Christians, we are always on the opposite side of the majority. But when a believer makes a righteous stand for God, God allows us to experience his unmerited favor.

Mary the mother of Jesus was born in Nazareth. History states that Nazareth was known to be a place of ill repute. The people there were lax in their morality. Yet, despite this lack of standards, Mary did not let societal norms affect her choices to do what was right in the sight of God. The effects of her right living can be found in Luke 1:28. An angel was sent to proclaim that she was "highly favored, the Lord was with her, and blessed was she among women".

What did that mean for Mary and us as believers today? If we dare to be holy in the midst of an ungodly people, we will be compassed or surrounded with favor. This partiality results in God gracing our life in an unusual way.

There is no good thing that He will withhold from us if we walk upright before HIM!!

He did it just for me 

GRM by Nikki Crutchfield

Just a bit of good news! No one loves us like Jesus.

Isaiah 53 gives us a poetic and demonstrative look at the love of God towards mankind and His response to the rebelliousness of man. God's ultimate reaction was to give His only son as a propitiation or a substitution for our sins.

Isaiah 53 further gives a 89vivid description of what Christ would endure prior to his death. He would allow:

> ~ *Himself to be crushed*
> ~ *Himself to be broken*
> ~ *Himself to be bruised*
> ~ *His honor to be violated*

Jesus concedes to be the ultimate sacrifice with full knowledge of what would take place. He was willing to be *"wounded for our transgressions;* "*bruised for our iniquities: and* [have] *the chastisement of our peace upon him……*"

In other words, Jesus endured in order for us to gain advantages from his sufferings. Our advantages include: removal of the guilt and penalty our rebelliousness causes, the freedom from individual distresses/sickness, and soundness of mind along with a conciliatory relationship with God.

Isn't it good to know….He died, just for us!

Nikki Crutchfield lives in Prince Georges County.
She divides her time between home, church, and helping
others write while writing herself.   Nikki has been married

for over 18 years to one affectionately known as "Brown Face". She has two sons, Damon and Deonte.